Opera Soufflé

OPERA
Soufflé

60 PICTURES IN BRAVURA

MARC SIMONT

HENRY SCHUMAN, INC.
NEW YORK

Programme

RIGOLETTO

LA TRAVIATA

LA BOHÈME

SAMSON ET DALILA

AIDA

L'ELISIR D'AMORE

Intermission

DIE WALKÜRE

PARSIFAL

LOHENGRIN

Opera Soufflé

Rigoletto

Act I scene i

ARIA: *Questa O Quella*

D U K E

"'Mongst the beauties here around, . . ."

Act I scene vi

The malediction

Act II scene xv

The abduction of Gilda

Act IV scene iii

The plot

Act IV scene ix

The pay-off

La Traviata

Act II

ARIA: *De' Miei Bollenti Spiriti*

ALFREDO

"Softly sweet with magic spell
She calmed my wild emotion; . . ."

Act II

"('Dear Alfred; by the time you receive this letter'—)"

Act II

<small>ARIA:</small> *Di Provenza Il Mar*

<small>GERMONT</small>

"From Provence, sea, and land, what made thee
e'er depart? . . ."

Act IV

VIOLETTA

". . . A vain delirium 'twas, 'twould seem,
That I could baffle fate; . . ."

Act IV

DR. GRENVIL

"She is dead!"

SMITH FRÈRES

NOIRE

PILULES POUR LA TOUX

La Bohème

Act I

SCHAUNARD

(pettishly)

"The devil fly away with you entirely!"

Act I

MIMI

"Excuse me, my candle's gone out."

RUDOLPH

"Is it?"

Act II

SCHAUNARD

(. . . he watches the crowd curiously)

"Surging onward—eager, breathless—
Moves the madding crowd,
As they frolic ever
In their wild, insane endeavor."

Act III

RUDOLPH

". . . With bosom swaying,
One foot displaying,
Doth she lure him on
With the magic of her smile."

MARCEL

"Shall I be frank? I think 'tis hardly true."

Act IV

MUSETTA

(hoarsely)

"'Tis Mimi—'tis Mimi who is with me—
And is ailing!"

Act IV

"(. . . The curtain slowly falls.)"

Samson et Dalila

AIDA

L'ELISIR D'AMORE

Act I

"(Abimelech, sword in hand, rushes at Samson to strike him down. Samson tears the sword out of his grasp and strikes him. Abimelech falls, crying out 'Help! Help!' The Philistines strive to succor him, but Samson, brandishing his sword, drives them away. He is on the left of the stage, and utter confusion reigns. . . .)"

Act II

DALILA

"Why dost thou turn thy face,
Beloved one? . . ."

Scene at left as seen from balcony seats B118, B120, and C118.

Aida and Memphians

Radames and Thebans

Amneris and Aida

Triumphant trombonist

Act III   scene ii

L'ELISIR D'AMORE

ARIA: *Una Furtiva Lacrima*

NEMORINO

"In her dark eye embathed there stood
Trembling, the furtive tear . . ."

Intermission

DIE WALKÜRE

Act I

SIEGLINDE

(meeting the questioning look of Hunding)

"Weak and worn
Found I this man:
Need drove him our way."

Act I

SIEGMUND

". . . A wolf-cub tells thee this tale,
Who a wolf to many has seemed."

Act II

FRICKA

(to Brünnhilde)

"War-lord, he
Waits for thee:
He will inform thee
How his lot he has cast!"

Act II

WOTAN'S VOICE

"Back, back! from the spear!
Down, down! with thy sword!"

Act III

WOTAN

" . . . Farewell! Farewell! Farewell! . . ."

Parsifal

Act I

GURNEMANZ

". . . A dolt so dull
I never found, save Kundry here."

Act II

"(The figure of Kundry gives forth a sudden shriek
of anguish. . . .)"

Act II

"(. . . a youthful female of exquisite beauty—Kundry, in entirely altered form—on a flowery couch and in light drapery of fantastic, somewhat Arabian style. . . .

She has bowed her head quite over his, and now presses her lips on his in a long kiss.)"

Act II

KLINGSOR

(poising a lance)

"Halt there! I'll ban thee with befitting gear: . . ."

Act III

GURNEMANZ

"Greet thee, my friend!
Art thou astray, and shall I direct thee?"

Act III

Procession of the knights

LOHENGRIN

Act I scene iii

Lohengrin, King Henry the "Fowler," and Thuringians

Act III scene ii

Foiling the plot of Frederick, Count of Telramund

Curtain call. Lohengrin, Ortrud, Elsa, Frederick